COUNTERING THE VIRTUAL CALIPHATE: THE STATE DEPARTMENT'S PERFORMANCE

HEARING

BEFORE THE

COMMITTEE ON FOREIGN AFFAIRS
HOUSE OF REPRESENTATIVES

ONE HUNDRED FOURTEENTH CONGRESS

SECOND SESSION

JULY 13, 2016

Serial No. 114–205

Printed for the use of the Committee on Foreign Affairs

Available via the World Wide Web: http://www.foreignaffairs.house.gov/ or http://www.gpo.gov/fdsys/

U.S. GOVERNMENT PUBLISHING OFFICE

20–744PDF   WASHINGTON : 2016

For sale by the Superintendent of Documents, U.S. Government Publishing Office
Internet: bookstore.gpo.gov   Phone: toll free (866) 512–1800; DC area (202) 512–1800
Fax: (202) 512–2104   Mail: Stop IDCC, Washington, DC 20402–0001

COMMITTEE ON FOREIGN AFFAIRS

EDWARD R. ROYCE, California, *Chairman*

CHRISTOPHER H. SMITH, New Jersey
ILEANA ROS-LEHTINEN, Florida
DANA ROHRABACHER, California
STEVE CHABOT, Ohio
JOE WILSON, South Carolina
MICHAEL T. McCAUL, Texas
TED POE, Texas
MATT SALMON, Arizona
DARRELL E. ISSA, California
TOM MARINO, Pennsylvania
JEFF DUNCAN, South Carolina
MO BROOKS, Alabama
PAUL COOK, California
RANDY K. WEBER SR., Texas
SCOTT PERRY, Pennsylvania
RON DeSANTIS, Florida
MARK MEADOWS, North Carolina
TED S. YOHO, Florida
CURT CLAWSON, Florida
SCOTT DesJARLAIS, Tennessee
REID J. RIBBLE, Wisconsin
DAVID A. TROTT, Michigan
LEE M. ZELDIN, New York
DANIEL DONOVAN, New York

ELIOT L. ENGEL, New York
BRAD SHERMAN, California
GREGORY W. MEEKS, New York
ALBIO SIRES, New Jersey
GERALD E. CONNOLLY, Virginia
THEODORE E. DEUTCH, Florida
BRIAN HIGGINS, New York
KAREN BASS, California
WILLIAM KEATING, Massachusetts
DAVID CICILLINE, Rhode Island
ALAN GRAYSON, Florida
AMI BERA, California
ALAN S. LOWENTHAL, California
GRACE MENG, New York
LOIS FRANKEL, Florida
TULSI GABBARD, Hawaii
JOAQUIN CASTRO, Texas
ROBIN L. KELLY, Illinois
BRENDAN F. BOYLE, Pennsylvania

AMY PORTER, *Chief of Staff*   THOMAS SHEEHY, *Staff Director*

JASON STEINBAUM, *Democratic Staff Director*

CONTENTS

COUNTERING THE VIRTUAL CALIPHATE: THE STATE DEPARTMENT'S PERFORMANCE

WEDNESDAY, JULY 13, 2016

HOUSE OF REPRESENTATIVES,
COMMITTEE ON FOREIGN AFFAIRS,
Washington, DC.

The committee met, pursuant to notice, at 10:01 a.m., in room 2172 Rayburn House Office Building, Hon. Edward Royce (chairman of the committee) presiding.

Chairman ROYCE. This hearing will come to order. Today we continue our oversight of the administration's response to ISIS and to Islamist extremism. Specifically we will be looking at the State Department's effort to counter ISIS' message online.

As the committee heard last month, the Internet is awash with terrorist propaganda and this includes horrific videos of beheadings, of firing squads, of torture of men, women, and children. ISIS operates a vast network of online recruiters; online propagandists. The mission of these individuals is to expand their ranks across multiple continents, including our continent, including right here at home.

So this is on the Internet, what would be called their "virtual caliphate." They use popular media sites, and through that process ISIS can reach a global audience—it does this within seconds. Once lured in, they communicate privately on platforms with sophisticated encryption encouraging tens of thousands—including many from Western countries—to travel to Syria, to travel to Iraq, to travel to Libya and join the fight. But more and more the virtual caliphate is calling on its followers not to take that trek to Syria or Iraq or Libya or other camps, terrorist camps that they have set up, but instead to attack where they are—to take up arms at home. That is the new messaging. And Orlando is a grim example of that.

As we will hear today, ISIS' online presence is just as critical to the organization as the large amounts of territory that it controls, whether that control be in Iraq or Syria or Libya. Defeating ISIS on both the physical and virtual battlefields requires very strong, very decisive action.

Now in the past unfortunately the State Department effort to respond to extremist content online has struggled. Its Center for Strategic Counterterrorism Communications was designed to identify and to respond to extremist content online. Yet because its communications were "branded" with the official State Department seal, nobody listened.

(1)

In March, the President issued an executive order to revamp this effort, renaming it the Global Engagement Center. And Richard Stengel, our new Under Secretary for Public Diplomacy and Public Affairs, is here with us to testify today. It was given the mission to lead the government-wide effort to ''diminish the influence of international terrorist organizations.'' We look forward to hearing from the Department on how the Global Engagement Center is taking on this fight.

At a basic level key questions remain, including the type of message that would be most effective in the face of this virulent ideology. Some suggest that the voices of disaffected former jihadists are particularly potent in deterring future jihadists. These are individuals who quickly discovered that life under ISIS was not as advertised, is not the utopia that they were promised, and they have the skill to communicate just how disillusioned they were.

But if this is the message, how should it be delivered? Should the Federal Government produce and disseminate content? Is the Federal bureaucracy equipped for such a fast moving fight? I suspect not. Does any association with the State Department mean this message is dead on arrival? As one witness told the committee last month: ''Worst of all, Government is by definition risk averse which is the opposite of what you have to be online.''

Previous witnesses suggested that a more effective approach could have the U.S. Government issuing grants to outside groups to carry out this mission. This would have the advantage of allowing the U.S. Government to set the policy, but put those with the technical expertise and credible voice in the driver's seat. After all, such separation and distance from the U.S. Government has helped our democracy promotion programs through the National Endowment for Democracy, for those of us that remember their method of operation over the years. They work in areas of the globe where official U.S. support just isn't feasible.

And what role should technology companies play in all this? What about that sector? In recent weeks, some have announced promising new technologies that would automatically remove extremist content as soon as it goes online. We need everyone acting in sync, including the tech sector, including the entertainment industry, including the government.

Time is of the essence. If we don't come to grips with the virtual caliphate now, this struggle against Islamist terrorism will become more challenging by the day.

So I will now turn to the ranking member, Mr. Elliot Engel of New York, for any opening comments that he may have.

Mr. ENGEL. Thank you, Mr. Chairman. Thank you for calling this hearing. Under Secretary Stengel, welcome to the committee. I used to be a big fan of Casey Stengel. I don't know if he is related. I know the director of the Global Engagement Center, Michael Lumpkin, has briefed us there a couple of times and it is great to have you with us today. Thank you.

The development of information technology during our lives has dramatically changed the way people around the world communicate, share information, and conduct business. We are connected on a global scale like never before and so much good that can come of that. But we know it cuts both ways. This incredible tool can also be used for incredible harm and there is no better example of that than the way ISIS has harnessed technology to spread its hateful message and recruit more fighters into its ranks. With a click of a button ISIS can broadcast its shocking violence to virtually anyone with a laptop or a smart phone, and with social media ISIS works to radicalize people around the world urging so-called lone wolves to attack targets in their communities, urging terrorists to take full advantage of lax gun laws that make buying a weapon as easy as buying a secondhand baseball card.

Though we cannot spot it on a map, our efforts to confront ISIS' virtual violence is another major front in our Counterterror Campaign. In fact, this online battlefield may be ISIS' last stand. It was reported today that even ISIS terrorists realize their days are numbered when it comes to controlling large swaths of territory. That is why the group has shifted tactics, lashing out around the world, so as the coalition continues to reverse ISIS gains in Iraq we also need to focus on taking away this recruitment and propaganda tool.

The Obama administration began focusing on this problem years ago with the creation of the Center for Strategic Counterterrorism Communications, what we call the CSCC at the State Department. Diplomats and national security professionals were given the job of taking online space back from violent groups that had filled it with propaganda. The model followed our traditional approach to public diplomacy, speaking on behalf of the U.S. Government.

But an evaluation of these efforts after a few years showed us some areas that needed improvement. First of all, we needed better coordination with outside partners. Secondly, we needed to provide information from sources that the target audience would consider credible. And lastly, we needed to find a better way to determine whether our efforts actually help prevent radicalization.

These are real challenges, particularly the last one. It is virtually impossible to count the number of people who may have joined the terrorist group but then decided not to. To deal with these concerns, the administration created a new organization at the State Department called the Global Engagement Center which is designed to coordinate and integrate all of our counter messaging efforts.

It has moved away from direct U.S. Government messaging to partner-driven approach tapping a global network of NGOs, foreign governments, and individuals who can better deliver our message to the right audience. It aims to encourage ordinary people in at-risk communities to launch grassroots messaging campaigns of their own and it places a premium on cutting edge technology and top talent from the private sector.

So I firmly support this approach and I am glad my friends on the other side of the aisle do as well. The counter messaging provisions of the Speaker's new national security action plan echo the administration's strategy almost word for word. Both plans explicitly focus on empowering locally credible voices and employing new tools to effectively measure results.

And we are starting to see some good outcomes. It was reported yesterday that ISIS' Twitter traffic has dropped by nearly 50 percent in the last 2 years, so we are on the right track. The question now is how do we see this agenda through? How do we continue to refine our strategy, identify credible actors, improve our ability to measure results, and keep up with ISIS as its online campaign continues to evolve?

I personally think we should be investing a lot more money into this effort. Since 2013, the budget has jumped from less than $5 million to a 2017 request for $21.5 million. That is a good increase, but in my opinion we should go even farther.

I am curious to hear from our witness about what other steps the administration is taking to implement the current plan and keep building on it. I look forward to your testimony. I thank you, Mr. Chairman, and I yield back.

Chairman ROYCE. Thank you, Mr. Engel. So today we are pleased to be joined by Under Secretary for Public Diplomacy and Public Affairs Richard Stengel. And prior to serving in this position, as everyone knows Mr. Stengel was the managing editor of Time as well as the president and chief executive officer of the National Constitution Center in Philadelphia.

We are going to, without objection, ask that the witness' full prepared statement be made part of the record, and members here will have 5 calendar days to submit any additional statements or questions for the record that they might have and any materials.

And we would ask, Mr. Stengel, if you could summarize your remarks and we will have 5 minutes and then go to questions. Thank you very much.

STATEMENT OF THE HONORABLE RICHARD STENGEL, UNDER SECRETARY FOR PUBLIC DIPLOMACY AND PUBLIC AFFAIRS, U.S. DEPARTMENT OF STATE

Mr. STENGEL. Chairman Royce, thank you for that kind introduction. I am delighted to be here. And I want to thank you personally for your interest and support of public diplomacy. The 21st century is the public diplomacy century and your support is vital.

Ranking Member Engel, Chairman Royce, distinguished committee members, thank you for the opportunity to have me appear today to discuss the role of public diplomacy in countering violent extremism. This hearing comes at a critical time in our fight against ISIL and violent extremism.

In just the last few weeks, from Istanbul to Baghdad to Dhaka, we have once again seen the terrorists' wanton brutality and disregard for the lives of innocent people. Yet at the same time as we have seen these attacks the narrative is changing. There are signs of progress in our efforts to counter ISIL's message. The amount of anti-ISIL content on social media platforms is increasing, while ISIL's own content, as the ranking member mentioned, is decreasing. The virtual caliphate itself is shrinking.

Across the U.S. Government our strategy for countering ISIL in the digital world has become more coordinated and more effective. The tech companies as well have stepped up their efforts at our behest. I would like to outline a few of the steps we are taking, some of which you have heard about already and note at the same time that much needs to be done.

Now I think as folks know, this past fall we did an intensive review of what was CSCC, the Center for Strategic Counterterrorism Communications, which was formed in 2010 to fight a different enemy. That was al-Qaeda. But they saw that this new enemy ISIL was coming on board and we began to shift.

So we evolved into the Global Engagement Center with an executive order signed by the President, and that Global Engagement Center has two missions. One is to coordinate anti-ISIL and anti-extremist violent messaging within the government, and the second, again as both of you gentlemen have mentioned, is to enable third party voices—to optimize them, to amplify them—because their voices are more powerful against ISIL than ours. That is the core insight that made for this change—that our voice is not necessarily the best voice to be out there.

And now we see this, the tide turning. Now I am just going to take exception and back to something the chairman said in the beginning of the hearing, this idea that the Internet is awash with ISIL or pro-ISIL content. There is a RAND study that came out recently, it is confirmed by our own GEC study that there is now six times as much anti-ISIL content on the Internet as pro-ISIL content.

When I started in this job it was one to one. The tide is shifting. This idea that Twitter is awash with ISIL content, we did an analysis recently: 0.0124 percent of Twitter's content is pro-ISIL content. So—and these beheading videos that people talk about, every week I have a briefing about ISIL's top ten and I had a briefing yesterday and I asked to see any new videos. And the problem was is that the videos are being taken down so quickly that we don't even get to monitor them.

So I think this narrative that we are losing the information war with ISIL is wrong. In fact, mainstream Muslims are winning the information war with ISIL and that is why we have seen that great boost of content. So—but this issue faces public diplomacy all around the world. There is a digital iron curtain going up around the world. There is a gigantic increase in disinformation at the same time coupled with countries that are decreasing their free speech in their areas. This is a gigantic challenge for democracies and it is something I am happy to talk about as well.

We believe the most effective tool against this is the free flow of information and independent press, which we support. So this is long term and important work. I am happy to talk about it all. We will face setbacks I know, but I believe that we have embarked in the right direction and we have the right strategy. And I want to thank you again for having me here. I know we have been trying to do this for a while and I look forward to taking and answering your questions.

[The prepared statement of Mr. Stengel follows:]

STATEMENT OF RICHARD A. STENGEL

DEPARTMENT OF STATE

UNDER SECRETARY FOR PUBLIC DIPLOMACY & PUBLIC AFFAIRS

BEFORE THE 114th CONGRESS

U.S. HOUSE COMMITTEE ON FOREIGN AFFAIRS

JULY 13, 2016

10:00 AM

RAYBURN HOUSE OFFICE BUILDING

Chairman Royce, Ranking Member Engel, distinguished committee members - thank you for the opportunity to appear today to discuss the role of public diplomacy in countering violent extremism and provide an overview of how public diplomacy advances the strategic interests of the United States.

This hearing comes at a critical time in our fight against ISIL. In just the last few weeks, from Istanbul to Baghdad to Dhaka, we've seen again the terrorists' brutality and wanton disregard for the lives of innocent people. Yet, at the same time, there are many signs of progress in our efforts to counter ISIL's message. The amount of anti-ISIL content on social media platforms is increasing; ISIL's flow of content is diminishing and being interrupted. The revulsion to ISIL can be seen in the engagement of mainstream Muslims around the world who reject what the terrorists stand for. It can also be seen in the actions of the tech companies whose platforms are being used to disseminate much of this noxious content. They have ramped up their efforts to purge their platforms of this vile material and the content is often removed in minutes, not hours or days.

We must continue to focus on being more coordinated, more nimble, and more effective. My statement today will focus on messaging, but will also outline how we are harnessing the full range of public diplomacy tools to confront the challenge of violent extremism -- while recognizing the significant hurdles that remain.

This past fall, after an intensive review of our counter messaging strategy -- including consultation across the U.S. Government and with technology, marketing and communications experts from the private sector -- the White House and the Department of State announced that the Center for Strategic Counterterrorism Communications (CSCC) would be replaced by the Global Engagement Center (GEC), an interagency body housed at the State Department, reporting to the Secretary of State through the Under Secretary for Public Diplomacy and Public Affairs.

The Global Engagement Center has a dual mission: to coordinate, integrate, and synchronize government-wide communications directed at foreign audiences aimed at countering the propaganda of ISIL and other violent extremists; and to build the capacity of partners to develop content, amplify credible local voices and disseminate positive alternative narratives. Through these two lines of effort, the GEC seeks to disrupt and drown out ISIL's perverse narrative.

Our strategy is informed by a core insight: we are not always the best messengers for the message we want to deliver. Public statements from U.S. Government officials condemning ISIL can easily be used by the enemy as a recruitment tool. Our efforts focus on amplifying credible voices and lifting up those voices in a coordinated way – while assessing and measuring the impact of these efforts. The new approach is centered on "partner-driven messaging." Instead of direct messaging to potential ISIL sympathizers, much of our work focuses on supporting and empowering a global network of partners—from NGOs to foreign governments to religious leaders—who can act as more credible messengers to target audiences.

One example of our drive to build partnerships is the Sawab Center in Abu Dhabi, a joint messaging center where Emiratis work alongside Americans to counter ISIL online. Since July 2015, Sawab has launched nine original social-media campaigns, ranging from voices of victims and defectors, to affirming positive messages such as national pride. Each campaign has averaged over 125 million views on social media, and Sawab has consulted and shared its experience with 20 countries and international organizations interested in similar efforts to counter violent extremism online.

The establishment of Sawab has catalyzed U.S.-backed initiatives to support the creation of messaging centers in Jordan, Nigeria and Malaysia, where the Digital Strategic Communications Division is slated to open its new messaging center in Kuala Lumpur this summer -- a major step forward in US efforts to reach at-risk individuals in Southeast Asia.

To measure impact, the Global Engagement Center is using data analytics tools developed by Silicon Valley. These measurements allow the GEC to analyze foreign social media activity in near-real time and help our partners do the same.

There are signs of progress in the messaging space. According to recent RAND study, anti-ISIL content online outnumbers pro-ISIL content approximately 6:1. A GEC analysis has shown pro-ISIL messaging is down by 45% since June 2014.

We are pleased that many of the world's biggest social media companies, including Facebook and Twitter, have been proactively and voluntarily working to eliminate ISIL content from their systems based on their terms of service. In just the last year, we've seen marked improvement in these companies' reaction time and the volume of content that they are removing. We have established a regular and active dialogue with the technology companies to discuss our policy concerns.

What does success look like? The answer is something of a paradox. In the long-term we would like to see a media landscape that does not require U.S. government messaging at all, because NGOs, local governments, partners and credible voices are effectively drowning out ISIL's message of hate. Short term, we look for concrete signs of success -- which we are seeing – such as the reduction in the flow of foreign terrorist fighters and decreased media and social media activity.

Secretary Kerry has recently announced the expansion of the renamed Bureau of Counterterrorism and Countering Violent Extremism to coordinate the Department's CVE efforts and, along with USAID, introduced a new joint strategy to guide our collective CVE efforts. These changes reflect a larger reevaluation of how the State Department communicates in the 21st century.

People around the world today have more information at their fingertips every minute than their grandparents could discover in a lifetime. But the proliferation of information has created a dangerous by-product, the viral spread of disinformation by state and non-state actors. Countries like Russia and China engage in sophisticated media campaigns to either discredit credible news sources or create their own versions of reality. As Pat Moynihan used to say, you're entitled to your own opinions, not your own facts. But more and more in this age of disinformation, people and governments feel entitled to their own "facts." Even though there is more information than at any time in history, people seem increasingly unable to distinguish between fact and fiction. And this is exactly what some countries want. As journalist Peter Pomerantsev has said, "It's not an information war, it's a war on information."

The best defense in this information battle is the free flow of information. We don't defeat Russian propaganda by shouting louder than they do, or by trying to battle propaganda with propaganda. This is about the fundamentals of democratic society -- free speech and an independent press. We have increased our support to the journalists and civil society activists, empowering them to refute corrosive lies, highlight corruption, and support democratic institutions. This strategy to combat disinformation is part of our larger public diplomacy vision.

My two-and-a-half-year tenure as Under Secretary has convinced me that public diplomacy is a growth industry. Across the State Department, public diplomacy programs are now viewed as an indispensable part of our crisis-response toolkit. Our programming supports our strategic goals on issues ranging from countering ISIL to preserving peace, stability and respect for international law in the South China Sea to containing the spread of the Zika virus.

My team has expanded analytics, evaluation and research units that will bring new data to inform our strategies on every public diplomacy initiative. Our evaluation experts are focusing on the tools and programs that are most suited to achieving those goals, drawing on research on audiences, communication campaigns, behavioral science, and more. We are using data and research from both USG and private sector sources to help us enhance connections between foreign publics and the United States.

One of the U.S. government's greatest assets remains our power to convene. Last month, the President hosted the Global Entrepreneurship Summit at Stanford University, one of the best US government events I've participated in. Over three days 700 delegates from every region in the world pitched their ideas to the best business minds in America. Entrepreneurship, especially for women and youth, offers options to combat violent extremism, improves education, builds economies and gives hope to communities where it was previously lacking.

That power to convene is not limited by geography. Virtual town halls on Facebook and Google hangouts can be the modern day equivalent of the New England town hall. People around the world who want to engage with us may not always like our policies, but they have already shown a willingness to begin a dialogue with the United States.

A centerpiece of our public diplomacy strategy has been to cultivate and invest in the next generation of global young leaders. Our Educational and Cultural Affairs bureau has designed many critical exchange programs over the years to do this. In this Administration we launched the Young African Leaders Initiative and similar young-leader programs in Asia, Latin America, and Europe, to ensure we are providing a deeper understanding of the United States and our values. Our regional young leader initiatives convene extraordinary talent from across the globe; build powerful networks of thousands of youth influencers; scale businesses; expand skill sets; and create partnerships to tackle shared challenges. These initiatives also serve our strategic interests: the Young Southeast Asia Leaders Initiative, for instance, has bolstered the Department's push to strengthen an ASEAN identity and foster regional cooperation.

We also continue to expand opportunities within our flagship Fulbright Program, which is celebrating its 70th anniversary. Fulbright scholars, who are more diverse than ever before, are some of the best public diplomats our country has. Hundreds of Americans participating in Fulbright are helping to support English instruction around the world, and in doing so, are improving access to information and economic opportunity for hundreds of thousands of students in key partner countries and communities. Teaching English is a strategic investment that can pay huge dividends, which is why we are working with the Peace Corps and other partners to ensure our combined U.S. Government efforts in this space are attracting the best candidates and are coordinated to have maximum impact.

The lesson from these exchange programs is clear – we are long past the point where government communication can rely solely on reciting talking points from a podium. The world has moved into two-way conversations. Public diplomacy *is* a conversation. Our best partners in this endeavor are the American people: students, faculty and professionals welcoming visitors from abroad to study or do research – or conversely – Americans going abroad to study or engage foreign audiences. Citizen diplomats are more important than ever as we try to tell the story of who we are and what we stand for as a people and a nation.

I'm pleased to say that the Broadcasting Board of Governors, BBG, is adapting as well. In my role as the Secretary's delegated representative to the Broadcasting Board of Governors, I can attest to the impact a news organization can have when the right leadership is put in place and the old way of delivering information is reimagined. CEO John Lansing has done an incredible job in his short time. He is focused on building a modern media company that can use digital tools to deliver news across the BBG networks. Chairman Royce, thank you for your continued work and collaboration on improving the BBG.

With Congress and, specifically, this committee's support, public diplomacy benefits from distinct funding and authorities. It has always been my position that public diplomacy funding is linked to a comprehensive and unified strategy. This means that my responsibility is to work closely with Congress and this committee and staff to present unified budget requests and closely link spending plans and program reports.

Let me close by coming back to the issue of violent extremism. While the messaging battle against ISIL is showing signs of progress, we remain cognizant of the spread of ISIL ideology to other parts of the world. The work of public diplomacy is to build relationships in communities in every corner of the world so that people know they have a partner and ally in the United States. By being on the ground, by having our officers use their skills and talents to bring together seemingly disparate groups, we can begin to sow seeds of opportunity and resilience in places that would otherwise be susceptible to terrorist recruiting. This is long-term work and it will remain difficult. We know we will face setbacks, especially given the media space in which we operate. But after nearly two and a half years in this office, I am confident that we have the right strategy to accomplish our mission. Thank you again for inviting me today and thank you for your partnership in advancing the foreign policy goals of the United States. I look forward to answering your questions.

Chairman ROYCE. Well, I think you make a good point, Mr. Stengel. At the end of the day we have seen a quantum increase in the effort to push back. Part of the difficulty though is that when those messages get through from ISIS or ISIL, as we saw in Bangladesh, it apparently doesn't take that much breach into the society in order to be able to find those disaffected people or those who can be easily radicalized.

So even though we are mounting a more aggressive counter offensive, we still find the effectiveness of their ongoing drumbeat. And the reason for the hearing is to look at how we might better be able to counter in real time as I discussed the new programming that can be done on software that takes their sites down automatically. That is worth looking at.

Some of the concepts that you and I have talked about, engaging the tech sector in this, we have both had these conversations out in Palo Alto with allies in this effort who would like to be part of the solution. With advertising firms or with Hollywood or with others who have experience with writing a narrative or a counter narrative in order to offset ideology which is extremist.

So how can some of these come into play, I would ask? How do we reach out also to foreign media outlets? Are they receptive to running content on our behalf?

Mr. STENGEL. Thank you, Mr. Chairman. I share your concerns about this and I want to talk first about what you said about that their messaging is getting out there and it is being effective. I think again there is a misnomer about what they are doing. That somehow ISIL's messaging is so diabolically clever that they are taking nice young Muslim boys and girls and turning them into foreign terrorist fighters.

That is not the case. They are tapping into an already existing market of grievance and unhappiness that is throughout the Arab and Muslim world. They are sometimes pushing on an open door. Not only that but they are targeting young men and young women who have mental illness and who are psychotic. That is what we have seen in these so-called lone wolf cases.

So it is not so much that their messaging is so special and so good, it is that they are tapping into a market that already exists. I too share your belief, Mr. Chairman. That ultimately we win this information war through credible voices, through third parties, through Hollywood, through the kind of content that people who reject ISIL's dark ideology and that is happening.

I mean, as you know I went out to California recently. We had a meeting with the Sunnylands with content providers from the Middle East and from Hollywood. We came up with an idea of a virtual writer's room where we helped them with their narratives, a film festival. I took the secretary out there. We met with the heads of all the major studios. As someone said we have never been in the same room before except at the Oscars.

So we are trying to enable that. And I think using software as you mentioned, the tech companies have been actually very, very diligent, very, very aggressive in this area taking down content. Twitter itself said recently they have taken down more than 125,000 handles. They are all out there taking content off their platforms.

Chairman ROYCE. Yes. Yes. I have a question on a related issue and it has to do with an initiative, Under Secretary Stengel, that kind of caught me by surprise in terms of some of my colleagues on the Senate side.

Now as you have lain out, the Global Engagement Center is focused on ISIL. It is focused on international terrorist organizations and that is what we have been working on and that is where your focus is. That is a difficult task enough. Some would like to see the GEC's mission expanded to include all foreign propaganda, such as the disinformation coming out of Russia.

I am somewhat hesitant here because we have a mission in front of us that you are engaged on. Where are the efforts and resources of this new office that you have set up best focused, and are the threats to U.S. national security from state-sponsored propaganda that might come out of Moscow or Beijing, and on the other hand violent extremism messaging from groups like ISIL or Hezbollah, are those similar enough that they can be addressed by the same organization or with the same set of tools? If not, which Federal agency should lead in responding to each of these challenges? To me they seem very different.

But I would ask you, you know, between your office at the Department of State, the Global Engagement Center, and the Broadcasting Board of Governors, which organization has the lead in communicating with foreign audiences and how are policy messages communicated to each? This gets into my question about this suggested alternative that has been put out there.

Mr. STENGEL. Thank you, Mr. Chairman, for that question which is very broad and what I will try to do is go from the micro to the macro. You talked about the resources of GEC. We have tripled GEC's budget. But most of their money and expertise goes to trying to amplify and help and give greater credibility to those voices out there in the region.

They are helping to create content. They are helping to disseminate content. Not always in their own name. As you saw, as you mentioned early on, CSCC's problem was partially that it was government branded content. We have seen the metastization of ISIL to their so-called provinces and we are creating content. We have two Hausa speakers at GEC who are creating content to fight against Boko Haram in Nigeria. So we see this growth of the digital caliphate to the provinces and we are combating that too.

So you mentioned this idea of a larger disinformation center. I mentioned this rise in disinformation around the world as a problem. I think it is an interesting idea. I think sometimes people think because disinformation is on the same platform that all disinformation is equal. I don't think that is the case. I think what Russia is doing is different than what ISIL is doing. I think it is an interesting idea to explore for the next administration, and where that would live I am not sure.

But I do feel that in our public diplomacy realm between the GEC, between the BBG which you have been so supportive of, we have big battalions of people that can help. I have 700 public affairs officers around the world. Our posts help with all of these things too. So it is a very good question and one that I am happy to continue talking to you about.

Chairman ROYCE. Yes. I just think in terms of trying to put it all in the GEC, I think under the proposal that I heard GEC's mission would become far too broad for us to focus, really, on the issue at hand that they have been given right now which is to, you know, take down this virtual caliphate or the attempts by ISIS or ISIL to continue to recruit.

So—but I appreciate your thoughts on it, and I should turn to Mr. Eliot Engel of New York. My time is expired.

Mr. ENGEL. Thank you, Mr. Chairman. The administration's strategy for countering violent extremism and Executive Order 13721, which created the Global Engagement Center, both call for empowering credible third parties to counter ISIS' messaging online. I think that is good, the right approach and there seems to be broad support for it, but actually identifying and empowering these credible voices, I think is easier said than done.

So let me ask you, what do you look for in a credible voice? What tools do you use or will you use to assess whether it is actually credible in the eyes of our target audience?

Mr. STENGEL. It is a very good question, Ranking Member Engel. And one of the resources that we use, that I mentioned to the chairman, are our posts around the world who our locally employed staff there as well our Foreign Service officers who are dealing with local groups throughout the Gulf, throughout the Middle East, throughout the Horn of Africa. They help us determine who is a credible voice that we might want to work with.

At the same there are people that we have worked with for a while. As you know we created the Sawab Center with the UAE in Abu Dhabi. They work with local voices. We work with them. We are creating a messaging hub as well in Kuala Lumpur with the Malaysians. They are looking for local people as well. And these are people who have knowledge of Islam, who have knowledge of ISIL on the ground, who have credibility too because in part they haven't always been supporters of the United States.

So we are looking for people who are effective in that information war with ISIL. We started a defector's campaign which was the voices of young men and women who had been to the caliphate and came back and said it is not what it is cracked up to be. The engagement on that campaign eclipsed anything that we had done before.

Mr. ENGEL. And we are still continuing to do it.

Mr. STENGEL. We are. A group of partners is doing another one this fall. We have done campaigns about governance. We have done campaigns about ISIL's brutal treatment of women. This campaign model, which was an evolution of what CSCC did which was more direct tit-for-tat messaging, that campaign model we have discovered is much, much more effective.

Mr. ENGEL. And do you have the resources to do an adequate job? I know everybody can always use more money, but are your resources adequate?

Mr. STENGEL. Well, as you know, Congressman, I ran a media company once upon a time and frankly I had a lot more resources running Time than I have running the GEC. I also want to mention that I am not running the GEC, coordinator Michael Lumpkin, who the chairman mentioned, is running GEC and he is doing a terrific job in terms of really changing its focus, giving it momentum which he has.

So even though we have tripled the budget it is from a very small base. When I came in CSCC's budget was only $5 million a year. So I actually think the GEC under Coordinator Lumpkin's leadership could actually use more money and be more effective.

Mr. ENGEL. Thank you. At our hearing on this issue in June, we had a panel of nongovernmental experts who discussed two different approaches to identifying credible voices. Some experts have suggested a top-down approach using American media professionals to develop content and create messaging for third parties to disseminate. Others propose a bottom-up approach that would encourage Internet users from around the world to produce their own messaging through YouTube contests and other outreach.

This bottom-up approach could generate a lot of content for very little cost. It wouldn't all be effective, but some of it I believe would be exceptional and authentic. What do you see as the advantages and disadvantages of each approach, and in your view what is the most effective role of the U.S. Government in supporting these approaches?

Mr. STENGEL. Thank you for that question. As with so many questions like that the answer really is all of the above and both, both top level and lower level. But as I mentioned in my opening statement, the fact that there is now six times as much content on social media that is anti-ISIL as pro-ISIL is really a tribute to those grassroots voices, the voices of mainstream Muslim men and women who are repulsed by ISIL's vision. They are creating that content.

We are helping some groups that are doing that. We are trying to give capability to both individuals and groups, and to me that is ultimately where that battle of narratives will be won when those regular voices dominate. At the same time, you know, we can help give them greater capability, help streamline their message. I have talked to the people at different Islamic universities in saying here is how you shorten a 68-page fatwa to three different tweets. That is more effective.

Mr. ENGEL. I guess my time is up, Mr. Chairman, so—well, the one question I would ask is I would ask you about large social media platforms like Facebook and Twitter. They do play a prominent role in the radicalization process, so how do we work with these companies to combat radicalization? We have seen social media companies improve content removal, but what more should these companies do to support counter messaging efforts?

Mr. STENGEL. Yes. I mean their platforms, they do not support radicalization obviously, their platforms hold content that does preach radicalization. But I think the story of the social media companies and the tech companies is an underwritten story. They are all aggressively out there getting content off their platforms. As one of them said to me, this is our ecosphere. We don't want to have it polluted with this kind of noxious content.

So 2 weeks ago I was out in Silicon Valley. I was with the Secretary of State. We met with Mark Zuckerberg at Facebook about what they are doing. They have dozens and dozens of people, Arabic speakers, 24/7, taking down content. As I mentioned, Twitter has publicly said that they have taken down more than 125,000 handles.

When I was out there last year I met with a YouTube executive. I see these videos are taken down now within minutes where it just has 25 or 50 views, whereas a year ago they were up for minutes or even hours. So I think the tech companies are really aggressive in this space in ways that people don't always realize.

Mr. ENGEL. Well, that is good news and thank you for your efforts.

Mr. STENGEL. Thank you, sir.

Chairman ROYCE. Mr. Dana Rohrabacher of California.

Mr. ROHRABACHER. Well, thank you very much. And Mr. Under Secretary, it is very good to hear that we actually are making headway in something that is very vital to our security and the safety of ordinary people throughout the world against this radical Islamic philosophy that seems to have gained a certain amount of strength and power over these last few years which threatens normal people whether they are Muslims or Christians or Jews or whoever they are. So it is very good that you have been on top of this and had some positive things to report to us today.

Let me ask you a couple questions about, not necessarily what we are against on the Internet, but what we are for and what we have promoted. The counterpart to this growth of a movement that is intolerant and preaches hatred and repression of other faiths, we have people who are heroic people in the Muslim world. General el-Sisi now having been elected being President el-Sisi of Egypt, for example, is a pivotal character in the Middle East and actually in the world.

If Egypt would in some way, let's say, turn into a country dominated by those who would have a caliphate and those who would have the same type of controls and monstrous policies that ISIL has been promoting we would see a—that would destabilize the entire region, and I doubt if any other of the smaller governments would survive if Egypt became a radicalized society.

Are we doing something to promote those people for example in Egypt who, the clerics that have for example gotten behind President el-Sisi? President el-Sisi himself has reached out to Christians and other faiths. I might add one of the first leaders to do so. But have we done anything—I understand that actually there are more attacks on the administration in Egypt than there are as we say recognitions of the positive steps that he has made.

Mr. STENGEL. Congressman, thank you for that question. And of course I share your belief and understanding of Egypt's pivotal role in the Middle East and how so many countries in the Middle East look to Egypt for guidance.

Another area where people look to Egypt is their expertise in Islamic studies. So we have worked with Al-Azhar University in Egypt to try to help get the message that ISIL is anti-Islamic, that it is a perversion of Islam out in a way on platforms that they traditionally don't use. I mean, you know, having a book on paper is not going to get as much reach as being on social media.

So we have also worked as I mentioned with other countries in the region. We started the Sawab Center with the Emirates and we—and the idea of the Sawab Center is that we will create a network of networks and they will loop in other countries who share the revulsion with ISIL. So the Sawab Center is already working with members of the coalition, including Egypt on counter ISIL messaging.

Mr. ROHRABACHER. Well, that is—thank you very much for giving us some positive news. Let me ask you this about the methodology that we would use in approaching this. There is a big controversy as to whether or not the Muslim Brotherhood should be declared a terrorist organization. Are we in some way working with the Muslim Brotherhood in terms of the Internet and communications and the type of activities that you are talking about, or have we put that as to one of the groups we won't work with?

Mr. STENGEL. That is outside of my purview, Congressman, and I am happy to go back and talk to the Middle East Bureau or NEA about that question. But to my knowledge we are not doing any kind of joint messaging with the Muslim Brotherhood.

Mr. ROHRABACHER. Let's just note that there has been a lot of, how do you say, hesitancy if not outright opposition in the administration to efforts to try to come to grips with what the Muslim Brotherhood is all about. And after looking at the Muslim Brotherhood we know that it doesn't advocate violence itself, but it seems to lay the intellectual foundation for ISIL and other radical, just radical Islamists which then leads the radicals who have been captured by that philosophy to believe that they can have a caliphate and they are going to wipe anybody else out who doesn't agree with it. So it actually in the end causes there to be violence based on a philosophy that leads to that end.

So I would hope that we, while we debate whether or not it should be, the Muslim Brotherhood should be declared a terrorist organization, at the very least we should be very weary of having Muslim Brotherhood advocates laying the intellectual foundation for the debate on ISIL and other movements in the Middle East. So I thank you very much and I appreciate the positive report that we got today.

Mr. STENGEL. Thank you, Congressman.

Chairman ROYCE. Thank you, Mr. Rohrabacher. Mr. Brad Sherman of California.

Mr. SHERMAN. I want to thank you for your efforts. Our failure to deter terrorists is seen in San Bernardino and Orlando, and of course people will ask, well, why weren't we 100 percent successful? But we will never know how many young men were turned away from terrorist acts perhaps here in the United States by your efforts.

I am very pleased to hear you praise the media companies. It is good to know that they are helping. This was not the case a year and a half ago. In particular, you mentioned Twitter has taken down 125,000 handles, perhaps even more. This committee was very involved in pushing Twitter back a year and a half ago, and I hope I can add for the record our letter of March 6th signed by the ranking member, the chairman and some other members of this committee sent at a time when Twitter had a very different policy.

And I have a question that I hope you will respond to just for the record and that is, can you identify some social media companies that are not exemplarily helpful or extraordinarily helpful in their efforts, including those that are based abroad? Not every social media company is in Northern California.

I was pleased to talk to you before the hearing and learn that you have on your staff a gentleman who has done some graduate work at Al-Azhar. Many on the committee have heard me talk about the need for incredible expertise in Islamic theology and jurisprudence, but I hope that you will go further beyond someone who has done some graduate work at Al-Azhar to a graduate to a professor or someone qualified to be a professor at Al-Azhar and its Shiite counterparts.

I know that such a person might not pass the Civil or Foreign Service examination, so please let us know whether you have the flexibility to hire such a person. And not just a Schedule C, which is a temporary job. You need to be able to offer people more than a temporary job.

You point out that grievance opens the door. Everybody has a grievance. And there are those in the Muslim world who will say it is not enough, that it is outrageous that Israel exists where Muslims once ruled, but Al-Andalus also must be returned to Muslim rule that being Portugal and Spain. So there will always be a grievance as long as there are churches in Spain.

But these are psychotic people. They get to kill and rape and engage in pedophilia, get applauded for it on earth and be told they are going to heaven for it. They need to be branded as people who use piety as an excuse for their psychopath.

We have moved from broadcasting to narrow casting to chats, where you need thousands of people conversant in what potential terrorists are thinking. There are thousands of American Muslims who I think would help you if you called upon them to help you. But you have to do more than just ask them. You have to provide them some guidance. Not all of them are tech whizzes. Not everybody who wants to help you is under 30.

But also, and this is something where you can, or somewhere in the U.S. Government perhaps your office can be extraordinarily helpful, and that is a way to register as a trusted blogger. Because I go to my friends and they have talked about this. They say, now let me get this straight, Sherman. I am supposed to spend—I have a Muslim name. I am a practicing Muslim. I am supposed to spend hundreds of hours in terrorist chat rooms. What happens when someone knocks on my door and looks at my hard drive?

And I say, well, I will vouch for you. And they say, yeah, Sherman, clever. That is your way to make sure that you always have to reelected, because as soon as you can't vouch for me how am I going to explain that hard drive?

So I would hope that you would create a program where people can perhaps provide copies. I don't know if you will get a chance to read them, but at least get copies of everything they are putting in. But can some way identify themselves as on the right side, because otherwise I can't advise my friends to have these sites on their hard drive.

And finally, I hope you work with and—well, why don't I let you comment on that and——

Mr. STENGEL. Good. Thank you, Congressman Sherman, for that question and we touched on some of this in speaking before the hearing. All of the social media platforms have opportunities for individual users to flag content that violates the terms of service of those companies. The terms of service are their constitutions.

And they also have so-called trusted flagger systems where if you, Congressman, are a trusted flagger that complaint goes straight to a higher authority. In fact next week we have a meeting of all the anti-ISIL coalition countries and we are doing a presentation on that flagging service for those countries.

You asked about the tech companies that are not doing their fair share. In my experience everybody is alarmed about this. But one of the consequences of the effectiveness and aggressiveness of the tech companies on unencrypted platforms is that the bad guys are moving to encrypted platforms like Telegram, like WhatsApp, like Kik. And that is an area that the good news is that they are reaching a much smaller audience. The bad news is that we don't know what they are saying. So that is an interesting area for you all to probe as well.

Chairman ROYCE. Mr. Mo Brooks of Alabama.

Mr. BROOKS. Thank you, Mr. Chairman. Mr. Under Secretary Stengel, I was listening to your opening statement and you made an interesting comment and I hope I was able to write it down verbatim, something to the effect of that ISIS or the Islamic State is already "tapping into an already existing Muslim market." And then you mentioned I think grievance or anger or things like that. What did you mean by that already existing market?

Mr. STENGEL. I don't think it will come as a surprise to you, Congressman, or anyone on the committee, that in many of these places where they are searching out sympathizers there is high unemployment, there is lack of education, there are governments that don't necessarily value free speech. So there is this market of unhappiness that exists already.

I think now because the digital caliphate is shrinking they are looking for people who have mental health issues, who are psychotic, and they are trying to pinpoint those. But I think we are all aware that in terms of that, the Muslim world, there are places where there are unhappy youth although I am happy to say the Burson-Marsteller poll that came out a couple of months ago shows that 80 percent of the youth, 18 to 24, in the Middle East completely reject ISIL's ideology even if they became nonviolent.

Mr. BROOKS. Well, there are lots of places around the planet that have high unemployment, some degree of lack of education, some degree of unhappiness. What is it about Islam in particular that causes you to assert that that is an already existing market for terrorism as opposed to all these other places around the planet that have those similar characteristics but are not adherence to Islam?

Mr. STENGEL. Well, there is terrorism that goes by many different flags around the planet, not all terrorism is ISIL based. In fact one of the things that we have seen with the metastization of ISIL is that it has become a brand of convenience for people who have grievances that had not anything necessarily to do with ISIL's ideology.

And I should have said this in the answer to the first question. One of the other misconceptions is that ISIL's content is all negative and filled with beheadings. We estimate that 80 percent of their content is positive about the beauties and the joys of the caliphate and the duty of every Muslim to go to the caliphate. So for many people it is actually an inspirational message.

Mr. BROOKS. Where in the world is there the kind of terrorism that we have seen associated with Islam? Because you mentioned that there is terrorism around the planet, can you name anything that competes with or does as much damage as what was seen with the Islamic State in particular or say in America—Orlando, Boston, Chattanooga, San Bernardino and so forth? What other area of the world is so inspired to engage in these kind of organized terrorist barbaric acts of murder?

Mr. STENGEL. No, I would, I certainly agree with you that ISIL's terrorism and the effect that they are having is having the largest share of the market and the largest share of concern.

Mr. BROOKS. Have you ever read the Quran?

Mr. STENGEL. I have not read the entire Quran, but I have certainly read pieces of the Quran and have studied the Quran, yes.

Mr. BROOKS. Let me share with you why there might be an already existing Muslim market for this kind of terrorism that you referenced early on, and these are quotes from the Quran: ''When the Lord inspired the angels saying, I am with you, so make those who believe stand firm. I will throw fear into the hearts of those who disbelieve, then smite the necks and smite of them each finger. That is because they opposed Allah and his messenger. Who so opposes Allah and his messenger, for him, lo, Allah is severe in punishment.'' And that is Quran 8-12.

Then, ''Then when the sacred months have passed, slay the idolaters wherever you find them and take them captive and besiege them and prepare for them each ambush. But if they repent and establish worship and pay the poor-due, then leave them their way free. Lo, Allah is forgiving and merciful.'' That is Quran 9-5.

And then, ''The hypocrites and those in whose hearts is a disease and the agitators in the city do not desist, cursed. Wherever they are found they shall be seized and murdered, a horrible murdering.'' That is in Quran 33-60 through 62.

Is that what you mean by an already existing market for terrorism?

Mr. STENGEL. One of the things that I have seen that Islamic scholars say about the perversion of ISIL's ideology about Islam is they cherry pick passages from the Quran and from the hadiths, which as you know there are 200,000 hadiths, and it is pretty easy to find hadiths or parts of the Quran that may contradict each other and you have to look at it in context. I don't know the larger context of the passages that you mentioned, but one of the issues that mainstream Islamic scholars say is that they, ISIL perverts Islam by cherry picking these passages that seem to support its ideology.

Mr. BROOKS. Thank you for your insight.

Mr. Chairman, thank you for the time.

Chairman ROYCE. Ami Bera of California.

Mr. BERA. Thank you, Mr. Chairman, and thank you, Secretary Stengel. You know, in your opening comments you talked about two broad goals that you have in terms of coordinating anti-ISIL message and then amplifying the voices of the third parties that are trying to coordinate and counter the ISIL message. I would like to focus a little bit on that second broad goal.

I do think broadly in the United States as well as across the Muslim world, the vast majority of folks reject ISIL's message and want to counter that. That said, you know, their mechanisms of using social media and communicating in real time and building the message, you know, the imams may not be very adept at using social media, right. They may go on a blog and—in our prior hearing we talked about some of the difficulties that traditional anti-ISIL Islamic groups and third parties who want to counter may not be adept at, you know, countering in real time that message, building that relationship.

And what are some strategies that we can use along with technology companies that understand how to use these newer technologies to make them more effective in countering the message?

Mr. STENGEL. Yes, Congressman, thank you. It reminds me of the famous Mark Twain quote about the lie going around the world in the time that it takes the truth to tie its shoes. That the truth being these mainstream Muslim clerics who take the time to read the Quran, take the time to read the hadith and don't necessarily have an expertise in social media the way some of the bad guys do.

So one of the ideas that we have discussed and the chairman alluded to it earlier is, is there a private sector foundation or NGO of content creators, people who can help content creators, who can help the imam in Detroit to get on Twitter, who can help some of these voices get out there? Because what we have seen, and I have seen this in the Middle East, there is often a reticence among the good guys to be out there and we need to get them out there and we need to give them the skill set to be out there.

Mr. BERA. And as someone who is not of the—you know, when I think about my daughter or think about our younger staff members, they will roll their eyes when I talk about how I communicate on social media because it evolves so quickly. And I think it is more than just training those scholars and third party individuals, but it is probably partnering with them to take those messages and in very real time continually communicate and counter ISIL messaging in real time, and using the same tools that ISIL probably is using better than we are.

So that would be one point. You touched on something else though that certainly is of concern and came up in our prior hearing as well. As Twitter starts to take down a lot of these handles, as Facebook starts to take down these messages, we are, as you alluded to previously, starting to see folks go to apps like Telegram that are much more encrypted and much more difficult to monitor. That is of certainly some concern, because as we are trying to counter a message those apps become much more difficult. What are some strategies that we might be able to work on?

Mr. STENGEL. It is an area that we are just beginning to explore, this migration onto encrypted platforms. And again as I mentioned, the good news about is they are reaching much, much smaller audiences, but they are using it as tools of violence and violent acts not so much about persuading according to the ideology.

And we also know, again not to be pessimistic about it that the ability to create encrypted platforms is something that is becoming more widespread itself so that people are going to be able to do that in the field. And I am happy to talk more about that in a different setting where it would be appropriate but I share your concerns.

Mr. BERA. Great. And then in my brief remaining time, in our prior hearing, you know, we are certainly talking about countering the message online, but in our prior hearing we also had a discussion about using traditional media tools, right, using Hollywood, using movies to counter a narrative. Again, you know, in the Middle East as well as in certain ethnic communities they will consume television, they will consume movies. And what are our strategies to continue to put out an anti-ISIL message, an anti-radical ideology message? And that is one that I certainly think we ought to be doing a little bit more.

Mr. STENGEL. Yes. I mean, as you know, Congressman, the most powerful and comprehensive platform in the Middle East is satellite TV. It is not social media. And just during this past Ramadan—which is like sweeps week for television—Middle East Broadcasting, which is led by a brilliant man named Ali Jaber, did a series called Selfie 2. Selfie 1 was a satirical, comedic exploration that satirized ISIL and made fun of ISIL. This Ramadan it was the most successful and the most watched program in the Middle East. This is the kind of thing that we applaud. We had Ali at a retreat at Sunnylands that I mentioned earlier for content makers from Hollywood and the Middle East, and that is the kind of thing that I think again will actually win this war of narratives.

Mr. BERA. Great. And I am out of time, I will yield back.

Chairman ROYCE. Scott Perry of Pennsylvania.

Mr. PERRY. Thank you, Mr. Chairman. Thank you, sir, for your attendance. I just want to hearken back to your initial statements and some curiosity. You have given us some good information, I think, this morning that gives us some hope that we can turn the tide on these folks in the digital arena, but there are also some things that concern me and at least I am curious about.

And maybe it is just that we pick up the narrative and we repeat the narrative without really thinking about it. When we say ''lone wolf,'' these folks that are engaged in this cause of theirs that attack Americans and attack all around the world, they are not lone wolves. They are not the Unabomber. They are not holed up in some cabin somewhere only to themselves. They are connected to a network where they were inspired and where they were urged on and commanded and supported. And I think we do potentially a disservice to seeing this for what it is if we consider them in the lone wolf context. And I would just urge you to maybe reconsider a different terminology for them.

And then it also concerns me or at least I am curious about the assertion that they are mentally ill. Because people that kill a bunch of other people that have no connection to them personally or there is no grievance, they are not in a war or something like that where one side is against the other so to speak, in the traditional sense they are mentally ill and I think we can make that leap.

But I would submit to you that—and I am going to give you a couple names. And there was also, you know, in regard to what Mr. Brooks said regarding unhappiness, unrest, economic unrest, social mobility, whatever you alluded to there that that is what drives these people. Al-Zarqawi, bin Laden, Zawahiri, Baghdadi, people of means, people of education, people of status in their communities, we are talking about billionaires, millionaires, doctors; these are people that lead this organization and this effort.

And sir, when we say they are mentally ill, again I think we cloud, potentially cloud our view of—these are people who are committed to their religious cause. Now whether we feel it is a perversion of Islam or not is a wholly other discussion, but they feel that the people they are killing are perverting Islam. And they are not, you know, I would say that they are not what we classically consider mentally ill. They know exactly what they are doing. They have their faculties about them and they are committed to a cause. And I just worry that and I am concerned that that narrative, that position potentially clouds our judgment on how to address these folks.

And I know I haven't asked you a question yet, but let me ask you this. You know, ISIS cells in Raqqa are directing training and operations specifically at targeting Americans and people in the West, right. So if you are not aware, Assistant Secretary Atkin, he did defer to a classified setting and you may want to do the same. But when he said we also have to respect—we are talking about shutting down the network, the ability to gain access to the Internet in Raqqa, Syria. He said we have to respect the rights of citizens to have access to the Internet and balance that even in Raqqa.

We don't want to be at war with these people, but these people are at war with us. I would think that shutting down the Internet or the access to the Internet in Raqqa where the headquarters of ISIS is would be a tactical and strategic consideration that would diminish their capabilities. What is your opinion about that?

Mr. STENGEL. Thank you, Congressman. I am going to begin by saying that I share your wariness and concern about the term ''lone wolf.'' I think it is a misnomer. I think it is a term that is in part created by the media because it is a cliche. One of the things that we have seen is that the idea that someone is self-radicalized by himself or herself almost doesn't exist. I had a very smart person say to me it is much more of a epidemiological model for radicalization, i.e., frequent, intimate contact over and over.

Everything we have seen with any of these so-called lone wolves is that it wasn't about being radicalized about content. It was they were being touched repeatedly over and over by particularly recruiters who were trying to get them to go down that road. So I share your concern about that.

One of the reasons in the—to go to your question in the diminution of content that is out there is our success on the military battlefield that early on a Brookings study estimated that there were as few as 500 of these ISIL fan boys, these hyperactive people on social media who were creating the lion's share of the content out there.

Basically with our success on the military battlefield of getting back almost 40 percent of the territory in Iraq that ISIL once held we are getting rid of a lot of those people who are creating that content. And we have plans which as you say might be better discussed in a different setting about how to, while not getting rid of regular people's access to the Internet, getting rid of some of these hyperactive ISIL fan boys' connection to the web.

Mr. PERRY. My time is expired. Thank you, sir.

Chairman ROYCE. Lois Frankel of Florida.

Ms. FRANKEL. Thank you, Mr. Chair. Thank you, Mr. Stengel, for being here today. I want to just ask about maybe just a little, an adjoining subject I will say which is, you know, we have been told that one of the recruiting tools of ISIS or ISIL was making sex slaves available to them and we know there have been thousands at least physically and there has been the use of the Internet.

We saw that—Mr. Chairman, we went to Tunisia. I think we saw some people, giving you some examples, if it is okay I am going to put this——

Chairman ROYCE. Without objection, we will submit it to the record.

Ms. FRANKEL. Okay, put them in the record. But I will just—this was an example I will show you. This was a young girl, I think she was 12, 12 years old, being sold by ISIL over the Internet. So my question to you is, if you know, is there continuing to be a prevalence of this issue? What are we doing to try to shut it down?

Mr. STENGEL. Yes, Congresswoman, I share your revulsion with ISIL's treatment of women and girls. It is unimaginable and speaks to exactly what their values are rather than what they say. My understanding is that it continues. It is actually relevant to the discussion we had about unencrypted versus encrypted platforms. They are using encrypted platforms for this slave trade. They are using the so-called dark web.

This is not something that happens on the social media platforms that we all know, it is something that happens behind that digital curtain that we talked about and it again is something that we are working on. Again happy to talk about it in a different setting.

Ms. FRANKEL. Are some countries more successful at stopping the virtual terrorism than others and could you explain why?

Mr. STENGEL. It is a very good question and I am more in the messaging business which obviously the ultimate goal is to stop the flow of terrorists and foreign fighters. There are certainly some countries that are more aggressive, more active, more willing in the messaging space which I think has a direct correlation in deradicalization.

And I mean, I have mentioned before the Sawab Center which is in partnership with the UAE. I mean, the UAE has been very, very forward-leaning in getting into this space but yet we have had conversations and relationships with the Jordanians, with the Egyptians. As I mentioned there is another center that we are working on with the Malaysians. We have talked to the Indonesians. Everybody understands that they have to be in the space now.

Ms. FRANKEL. Because there seems to be now, if the physical caliphate is being reduced, it sounds to me like the danger now is these inspired attacks.

Mr. STENGEL. Again it is a very good question and it is a very big concern. We make a distinction between inspired attacks and directed attacks. And the unintended consequence of destroying the physical caliphate, which by the way was the raison d'etre of ISIL in the beginning; that they were creating a physical caliphate. The unintended consequences of that is that they are spreading into becoming more of an insurgency group and a non-state terrorist group and that is extremely dangerous, as we have seen from San Bernardino to Orlando to Paris, and there seems to be a correlation between the physical battlefield being shrunk and their expansion into this terrorist insurgency battlefield.

Ms. FRANKEL. I want to make sure I have the correct terminology here. But directed and inspired, is the difference that one, the attacker comes to it on their own versus being recruited? I think you referred to attacks because somebody kept going after someone.

Mr. STENGEL. Right. A number of months ago, Muhammad Adnani, who is the alleged spokesperson for the so-called Islamic State, said that while we are being reduced on the physical battlefield, the caliphate is physically shrinking, so you should take the battle—don't come to Iraq and Syria. Take the battle to wherever you are and attack infidels wherever you are. And so those are not directed attacks but they are inspired by that kind of pernicious ideology.

Ms. FRANKEL. Thank you. I will yield back.

Mr. DUNCAN [presiding]. I thank the gentlelady. The chair will now go to Mr. DeSantis from Florida 5 minutes.

Mr. DESANTIS. Thank you, Mr. Chairman. Thank you for coming, Mr. Stengel. How would you define this term that gets bandied about ''violent extremism''?

Mr. STENGEL. I am sorry. Can you repeat the question?

Mr. DESANTIS. How would you define this concept of violent extremism?

Mr. STENGEL. I would define it as people who take a radical or extreme belief to the extreme of actually committing violence in its name.

Mr. DESANTIS. And when we are talking about violent extremism, what type of beliefs have we seen that lead people to commit those acts of violence?

Mr. STENGEL. What types of belief have caused them to commit the acts of violence? Again I would, and we have circled around this a little bit today. I would say that it is not so much a belief system or an ideology, but it is this recruitment by people who are trying to get people to commit violence in the name of an ideology or an idea that it doesn't necessarily espouse violence by its very nature.

Mr. DESANTIS. So I guess because I think it is important because some of the stuff you have outlined I think is good, but how you see the problem I think is important. So for example, when we hear about some violent extremists I get the sense from some people in the administration that somebody who is committing terrorism in the name of Islamic jihad let's say that they are really not doing it because of any type of religion. What they are doing is they are trying to co-opt religion to justify, but really their main goal is to just kill.

And so that is kind of one view. I would say it is a very narrow view. Or you could have another view which says these folks actually are motivated by an ideology and maybe it is not necessarily the same way that most Muslims in the world view the faith, but they honestly believe it and they think it is their religious duty to wage war against societies and individuals who don't or aren't willing to submit to that belief system.

So when you are approaching this how is it? Are these people whose main goal is just to kill and they kind of use religion as a convenient excuse, or do you see groups like ISIS, groups like al-Qaeda, other terrorist groups as being people who really are committed to militant Islam and believe that they are commanded to do this based on that belief system?

Mr. STENGEL. Congressman, I think it is both. I think we have seen both. I mean, one of the statistics that I didn't mention earlier is that there has been an enormous decline in the flow of foreign terrorist fighters. The DoD estimates that it has declined by 80 to 90 percent. One of the things that we saw with those for the most part young men who were becoming foreign terrorist fighters is that 80 percent of them had very little or almost no knowledge of Islam. Their attraction to being foreign terrorist fighters ranged everything from just wanting to kill to adventurism to publicity, and yet there were others who believed in this apocalyptic ideology. And so we see both.

But I think for the most part, particularly as the actual physical caliphate is shrinking, they are looking for people who are willing to commit violence for any reason. But I do think——

Mr. DESANTIS. But they, the ''they'' are people you would acknowledge who really are committed to the ideology, correct?

Mr. STENGEL. They are committed to that twisted ideology which embraces violence as a means to the end that they desire.

Mr. DESANTIS. So as you approach this how do you view, because I have seen a lot of different surveys down in the Islamic world where you have very high numbers of people who support the imposition of Sharia Law and which obviously has some very harsh consequences for women, for people who don't believe, who are non-Muslims, and what have you. The vast majority of those people I don't think would ever join a terrorist group, but they do believe in that kind of concept of civil society. Now you have the terrorist groups who want a caliphate under Islamic law as well.

So how do you deal with trying to reach people whose conception of civil society is radically different from ours but we don't necessarily, we want to give them an option other than just going into the terrorist camp? Because some of these people, if they believe deeply in Sharia and they have Western folks, and you did make a good point in your testimony about us not always wanting to be the messenger, but if they have messages that are coming, even though ISIS may not be their ideal cup of tea that may seem a little bit more attractive than if we are selling something that they think is contrary to their faith.

Mr. STENGEL. Congressman, it is a really difficult question and a really good one and philosophical one. And I am probably not supposed to mention people's books here, but I recently read a book called ''Islamic Exceptionalism'' by Shadi Hamid. And the thesis was that this separation of church and state that we have in the West and with Christianity, which happened over hundreds and thousands of years, isn't necessarily true of Islam. That Islamic law is intrinsic to being a good Muslim citizen, and this idea of a separation doesn't exist in Islam the same way it exists in the West and Christianity. I think that is an interesting and provocative point that needs to influence our policy and understanding.

Mr. DESANTIS. Great. I am out of time. I will just say I would like to submit a question about some of the clerics like Sheikh Qaradawi, very important with the Brotherhood, how we deal with the messages that they are sending. And I yield back.

Mr. DUNCAN. And I thank the gentleman. The chair will now go down to the gentleman from Rhode Island, Mr. Cicilline.

Mr. CICILLINE. Thank you, Mr. Chairman. Thank you, Mr. Secretary, for your testimony and for your extraordinary leadership and the progress that has been made under your leadership. I want to begin first with the level of financial support that Congress provides to your work.

When you consider the level of information that is being produced by violent extremists online I think you have already hinted at the fact that you could obviously do more with more resources, but I am going to ask you directly. Is the government adequately resourcing the Global Engagement Center to fully support its mission? From your experience what level of funding do you need?

And then the second part of the question is really what are other countries doing and what are the capabilities of other countries to engage in this fight and are there countries that should be doing more or do we have great partners? But the real first question is are we doing our part in terms of funding the work of your department?

Mr. STENGEL. Mr. Congressman, thank you for your——

Mr. CICILLINE. I mean as a comparison, in the U.K. for example the agency that deals with online counter messaging and anti-terrorist activities is funded at $8 million. So that is just a relative comparison. It seems like we are seriously under funding this effort.

Mr. STENGEL. Well, I thank you for that question and it is an issue that we discuss and think about every day.

I just want to pull back for 1 second and say that the GEC, as effective as it is, it is only 4 months old. It is one part of a constellation of things that we are doing, you know, not only public diplomacy issues but working with partners. I mean, you mentioned the British. We have worked with the U.K. to stand up the coalition Web site which tracks, in English, the successes of the coalition against ISIL. That is something we literally didn't have a year ago. So we leverage our partnerships and that has a dollar value as well.

But I do think, Congressman, and even though we have tripled the very small budget of CSCC into GEC, we have asked for, I believe, $21 million for Fiscal Year 2017, I think $60 million for Fiscal Year 2018. So we think we could do more with more.

Mr. CICILLINE. Thank you. Next I want to ask you about the work of sort of building the cadre of people who would be authentic, credible sources on social media to respond to Daesh and other terrorist organizations. I think we recognize that the United States Government is not the best provider of that content or to actually do it, and I am wondering what the other public diplomacy efforts that you are engaged in are doing to leverage that. For example, the exchange programs, the young leadership program, the Fulbright scholarships so that we can help build capacity and create those authentic voices who are then responding kind of organically to some of this in addition to funding, providing resources and building capacity of people who are already prepared to do it and are capable of doing it.

Mr. STENGEL. I am glad you asked that question. In fact I sent out a tweet yesterday about the beginning of the TechGirls exchange, which is bringing young Muslim women in STEM subjects to study here on exchanges. I mean, the exchanges are golden and transformational and frankly, you know, every dollar we spend in them I think we get much, much, much in return.

In that same vein we have IVLPs, international visitor leadership exchanges, in this area. We have increased the number of CDE IVLPs at my urging. And then we have also, we have something called TechCamps which was started in a previous administration but what I have beefed up and brought into public diplomacy. So we have doubled the number of TechCamps and I am doing it in this part of the world where we give people skills to combat that message in real time and they are often coupled with hackathons where they are actually creating contact.

Mr. CICILLINE. Great. And the final question is the FBI recently announced the Shared Responsibility Committees program, which offers an alternative path to intervention besides arrest. As you know, Canada and many of our European allies have a history of utilizing this deradicalization and intervention approach.

Have those been successful? Should we be, you know, developing similar deradicalization programs or should we be providing some additional emphasis on that approach? Has the history of that been effective?

Mr. STENGEL. As you know, Congressman, my focus from a statutory standpoint is on foreign audiences rather than domestic audiences. That being said, in my travels throughout the region, and I was at a conference in Jakarta on deradicalization, particularly in the Muslim Asia, the belief in deradicalization is something that is very powerful and they see it as something that jibes with this mainstream view of Islam.

And I do think it is something that we need to explore, that Americans need to know more about. And I don't have any data about success rates in North America, but it is something that frankly I would encourage a closer look at.

Mr. CICILLINE. Thank you. I yield back. Thank you, Mr. Chairman.

Mr. DUNCAN. The gentleman's time is expired. Thank you so much. I will now recognize myself for 5 minutes. Thanks for being

here. I would just ask the committee to remember Congressman
Ted Poe in our thoughts and prayers. Announced today he has leu-
kemia, and he is a valuable member of this committee, a valuable
Member of Congress, and a great American.

Mr. Under Secretary, I am on Homeland Security Committee as
well and been in Congress almost 6 years, and the Homeland Security Committee and the Department was formed after the 9/11
Commission really identified a lot of the walls that were put up between the sharing of information between agencies that led to some
of the failures that allowed the 9/11 attacks on America to happen.

But when I think about this as I am sitting here listening to the
testimony today, the Department of State has a Bureau of Counterterrorism and Countering Violent Extremism area. Now we have
the Global Engagement Center which was formerly the Center for
Strategic Counterterrorism Communications. So that is at the Department of State.

We also have the DoD which is using SOUTHCOM and
AFRICOM and other elements to combat terrorism globally, whether it is in this hemisphere or whether it is in Africa or whether it
is prosecuting the war against terrorism by dropping bombs and
drone strikes against actual ISIL and al-Qaeda elements throughout the war on terror.

We also in the country have the NCTC, National Counterterrorism Center. We have JTTFs, Joint Terrorism Task Forces, all
over the country working with law enforcement in the states. We
have the National Targeting Center which is looking at container
shipping and understanding how potential threats may transit the
globe.

We have an agency known as the Department of Homeland Security which was created, what, in 2003, 2004 which combined 22 existing agencies into one huge bureaucracy of all homeland security
elements whether that is, other than the FBI maybe that is a jus-
tice division, but NCTC, Secret Service, Border Patrol, Customs
and Border Protection, Immigration and Customs Enforcement,
USCIS, I could go through all 22 of them. There is a lot.

The reason I point out that is we have all these elements out
here within this huge bureaucratic United States Government that
are all trying to do the same thing and that is ultimately to keep
Americans safe and stop terrorism. Terrorism is a global effort
against freedom. To establish a caliphate is the goal of ISIS, but
there are other terrorist elements out there that are not involved
with ISIS. That is Boko Haram. That is Abu Sayyaf. That is Iran's
Quds Force. They are responsible for so many attacks on Western
elements.

So the question I have is we continue to change names and set
up different groups, how effective are we? And are we not creating
or recreating the problems we solved prior to 9/11 with all these
different groups? I guess what I am asking is there information
sharing or are there walls?

Mr. STENGEL. Congressman, thank you for that question. If you
recall, I came into government from the private sector and I think
I spent the first 6 months trying to memorize all the acronyms of
all the groups that I needed to know to be able to communicate
with.

Mr. DUNCAN. I didn't scratch the surface. I mean, as you know I didn't scratch the surface on the acronyms and alphabet soup of government.

Mr. STENGEL. That being said, I think one of the effects of 9/11 is that people realize that there were these silos of information and we weren't communicating. And the GEC by definition in the President's executive order creates it as an interagency body and an information coordinating body. So there are detailees from NCTC, detailees from DoD, detailees from the intelligence community, two detailees from Homeland Security at GEC that make up the staff.

And the idea is that by its very nature it is a coordinating entity to create coordination among messaging across the government, so I think to that extent it is doing a pretty good job of that. You know, it has been creating messaging coordination memos that go out to all of those folks. So I think we do both know more what everyone else is doing and we are beginning to do it together.

Mr. DUNCAN. What I am concerned with, Mr. Under Secretary, is that we are not being effective. And the reason I say that there are groups like Kronos Advisory, which is a private enterprise looking at global terrorism and they are monitoring not only social media, Twitter, Facebook, Instagram, you name it. They are also monitoring the dark web which I don't know that that element of the dark web and encryption has been brought up today, but ISIS is becoming a lot smarter. Social media is an easy way to attract those recruits. The communication is happening beyond the normal person's purview, not happening on Twitter.

So when I see a group like the one I just mentioned, a private group who can inform me as a Member of Congress and elements within the U.S. Government's intelligence service a lot faster about what they see on Twitter, what they pick up on social media than these alphabet agencies, I wonder how effective we are as a big government that is so seemingly disconnected.

And I think about the Department of State. I am sorry, but that is foreign relations. That is policies between governments. I don't really understand the Department of State's role in counterterrorism activities that I see the Bureau of Counterterrorism and Countering Violent Extremism. I am sorry, but I don't. I think that is a national security apparatus function with the Department of Homeland Security which I mentioned earlier, 22 agencies combined together to create this mega-bureaucracy as known as DHS. I wonder how effective that is being so large and cumbersome, but then I hear about the Department of State. I know what DoD is doing.

And my gosh, America just wants to be safe and they want to make sure we are all communicating. I think the gist of what I am asking today, and you don't have to answer this but the point I want to make is this. We don't need walls. We need to make sure that we are communicating. And I am not sure that large government agencies and the number of agencies that I mentioned all doing similar things is the most effective way, because sometimes smaller is better. Joe Montana proved that as quarterback of the San Francisco 49ers.

With that I will go down to Mr. Deutch for 5 minutes.

Mr. DEUTCH. Thank you, Mr. Chairman. And I want to thank the chairman and ranking member for making countering violent extremism a priority of this committee and appreciate the opportunity to engage with Under Secretary Stengel today. I would also like to associate myself with the remarks of the ranking member and so many others who have commended the administration for pursuing a strategy to combat ISIS and other terror groups online.

And I just wanted to follow up on a few points that have been raised here. One, with respect to social media, obviously, Mr. Stengel, it is not just that ISIS uses social media to recruit members and spread propaganda. After the shootings in Tel Aviv just weeks ago, Hamas took to Facebook to praise those attacks. Now the victims of Hamas' terror have filed a lawsuit against Facebook.

And I know as you point out that companies like Facebook have been aggressively getting content off of their platform and the peer-to-peer challenge that they have been actively engaged in I think also deserves great credit. The question is just a broader one and I would just like to start the conversation. Should a designated foreign terrorist organization be allowed to use U.S. based social media platforms?

Mr. STENGEL. Congressman, thank you for that question. And it is a large and philosophical question. And one of the things just to go down into the weeds for a second, in my conversations with the social media companies and in the trip that was publicized that was led by Denis McDonough to meet with the heads of the tech companies, one of things I hear over and over is we need help discerning one terrorist message from another. You know, is this a group that you might actually support as opposed to one that their content should be taken down? The intelligence community also creates messages that are sometimes confused for terrorist messaging.

So I think the tech companies are eager to collaborate with government about finding the kind of message that they want to take off their platforms, the messages that is polluting their platform. And as I mentioned they have their own constitution in terms of service and it isn't necessarily about designated terrorist organizations but the kind of content that is put up. And that is not something that we police, that is something that they police themselves.

Mr. DEUTCH. Well, it is and it isn't. I absolutely agree that they are policing content and they devote incredible resources to taking down content that violates their standards. But I really am getting at just the basic point of whether—and as I said it is a conversation I just think that needs to take place.

Referring to this specifically, is there a place, should foreign terrorist organizations be allowed to have a platform and I guess part of that conversation is, is there content—should we be making decisions and distinctions about the content on pages and sites, social media sites of designated foreign terrorist organizations or should we simply take the position that there is no reason to distinguish between something that is offensive and violates the standards of the company and something that I suppose may not technically violate the standards but still represents the words, the urgings of a terrorist organization?

Mr. STENGEL. If you are asking me, Congressman, no. I don't think a foreign terrorist organization should have a platform on any of these social media sites. That being said, one of the issues that we face all of the time is how the First Amendment applies to these American companies which is different than any other countries around the world.

As I mentioned earlier, so much of the ISIL content is actually positive. A few weeks ago I saw a tweet from an ISIL sympathizer and it showed a picture of a basket of apples and all it said was the caliphate is bounteous. Is that protected by the First Amendment or not? Is that content that Twitter should take off? I mean, I think these are very difficult questions and our environment on that continuum between freedom and security puts all of these things——

Mr. DEUTCH. I completely agree. I am sorry, because I am about out of time. But I think that is, and I don't know the answer but that is exactly the question. The question is are we doing less than we can if we allow terrorist organizations to post what would not be deemed, which would only be viewed as a positive post by anyone else? But to suggest that the caliphate is bounteous, it actually plays into a narrative that they are using to try to radicalize individuals around the world. I just think it is something we really need to struggle with and I appreciate the opportunity to start these exchanges with you here today. I yield back.

Mr. DUNCAN. I thank the gentleman. Especially when conservative content is deleted or denied and they allow radicalized content to remain up. I will now recognize Mr. Donovan from New York 5 minutes.

Mr. DONOVAN. Thank you, Mr. Chairman. I apologize. I have to be some place at 11:30. It is 11:40 already, so I am just going to ask quickly, Mr. Secretary, and I came to the hearing late so a lot of the questions were already answered.

I was very interested when you were saying how there is so much more anti-ISIS content online than there is—that surprises me—than there is pro-ISIS. Is that information, counter ISIS information things that our Government is putting online? Is that individuals putting online the anti-ISIS information and content?

Mr. STENGEL. Congressman, the lion's share of it is individuals and organizations and clerics and imams. It is not government messaging. Some of it is government messaging, some of it is government messaging of our partners. But as I say most of it is the voices of mainstream Muslims.

Mr. DONOVAN. And I know it is difficult to measure a negative, but is there a way? Can we tell how effective this anti-ISIS messaging is, the effect of it?

Mr. STENGEL. It is a very good question and it is hard to say. I mean, we do want to drown out their message with positive messages and positive narratives and that is something not just countering their message but providing alternatives. And I think one of the positives of that is that there are a lot of alternatives that are now being proposed and are out there.

Mr. DONOVAN. And I, like the chairman, am on Homeland Security as well and there was a debate, discussion on whether or not we should use folks who are radicalized who then have seen that the life they were promised was filled with falsehoods and whether or not we should use those individuals who want to explain to others that what you are being promised is not true, and I think that debate continues.

Let me just ask you quickly about the size of the recruits. I know you had also said that they are recruiting from a community of existing potential sympathizers and not expanding. I know some people are thinking that community of people of potential   recruits might be as large as 20,000 people. Do you have any idea about how big that community of potential sympathizers might be?

Mr. STENGEL. Well, the numbers that I have seen of the number of foreign terrorist fighters who have gone to Iraq and Syria from the very beginning is something on the number of 40,000, many of whom are killed, many of whom are gone. What I have also seen is a statistic from DoD that their flow every month used to be 1,500 to 2,000 and now it is 200 to 400. So it has been radically reduced, although that was a period quite a while ago in time so we don't know exactly what is happening today.

Mr. DONOVAN. And you answered my final question. I was going to ask you if you think that community is growing or shrinking and apparently it seems to be shrinking. Thank you so much for your time.

Mr. STENGEL. Thank you very much.

Mr. DUNCAN. The chair will now go to the former chairwoman of the committee, Ms. Ros-Lehtinen for 5 minutes.

Ms. ROS-LEHTINEN. Thank you so much, Chairman Duncan, and I had several conflicting events so I apologize if some of these questions have been asked before. I have several questions and pick which one you would like to answer within my time, sir.

As radical Islamist groups become more and more sophisticated we have seen them become more adept at manipulating social media platforms as tools to spread their propaganda, recruit vulnerable individuals to their cause, and extremist groups have found a way to adapt much quicker than we have been able to and they take advantage and exploit the rules we have in place in free societies that obviously protect privacy and speech. And that really seems to me to be the crux of the issue for Western societies.

How do we battle an ideology and a methodology that are not constrained by the same rules under which we operate? Individuals do not radicalize in a vacuum and I worry that our efforts   to counter message the existing narrative may already be lost before they begin. How effective can counter messaging work when it is likely that by the time we identify at-risk individuals they are already well on the path toward radicalization?

And here in the U.S. we have invested a lot in countering violent extremism programs like this and how do our programs compare to the efforts of our allies in the Middle East? Are they more effective than our own capabilities?

And also, a few weeks ago a team from my alma mater, the University of Miami, led by Professor Neil Johnson, published a study in the academic journal Science entitled, ''New Online Ecology of Adversarial Aggregates: ISIS and Beyond.'' And among its findings it found that pro-ISIS narratives develop through smaller, self-organized online groups and they have the ability to adapt, to extend their longevity, and even increase their numbers despite constant pressure from law enforcement groups and other anti-ISIS entities.

The study suggested that if these groups are not broken up at a fast enough pace then pro-ISIS support and material can expand exponentially faster through its networks. But it also suggested that anti-ISIS entities can use data mining and analysis to focus on taking down these hundreds of smaller groups before they get too strong. Are you familiar with this research, sir, and are you employing similar tactics at the Global Engagement Center?

And lastly, how effective is this Big Data mining and analysis when ISIS continues to adapt to employ techniques to avoid detection by the same people who are sifting through the information looking for them? Thank you so much.

Mr. STENGEL. Thank you, Congresswoman, for that question. And indeed you have touched on some of the things that we have talked about here today, but they are all very good questions. That is why it is so difficult in this space. The actual particular research that you mentioned I am not familiar with. I would very much like to——

Ms. ROS-LEHTINEN. I will send it to you. Thank you, sir.

Mr. STENGEL. Thank you very much. I have seen research that is similar about the distributed networks that ISIL has that they don't have a strong center. That these provinces and these other communication entities are distributed and they don't get a central message and that is one reason that it is difficult to compete with them.

Your point about the platforms is it is a difficult one. These are the greatest platforms for information in human history and they can also be abused by disinformation and this negative content. That is why we work so closely with those companies to help them get that content off their platforms. Those companies as much as we, maybe more, want to have that content off their platform because it ruins it for everybody else.

And the idea of Big Data is something that we want to explore. I didn't mention this earlier, but the GEC, the Global Engagement Center, is creating a Big Data hub, a data analytics hub, and it is using some tools from the interagency. There is a DARPA tool that they are using, Congressman Duncan that is worth mentioning. And so these are all issues that we are wrestling with and this is why it is a tough fight.

Ms. ROS-LEHTINEN. I fight that we must win. Thank you so much. Thank you, Mr. Chairman.

Mr. DUNCAN. Thank you. The gentlelady yields back. I will take the opportunity to tell you, Mr. Stengel, we appreciate your time today. You have been a great witness. And this issue is critical. That was pointed out by all the committee. You assert that the counter-ISIL message is gaining steam and look, I hope you are right. I think we all hope you are right. And as I noted, at the end of the day we are dealing with a huge bureaucracy, Federal bureaucracy that has its challenges.

So the committee looks forward to continuing the work on this effort and I look forward to continuing the work as a member of the Homeland Security Committee as well, and I look forward to us continuing to discuss this critical topic.

With no further business, we will stand adjourned.
Mr. STENGEL. Thank you.
[Whereupon, at 11:51 a.m., the committee was adjourned.]

APPENDIX

MATERIAL SUBMITTED FOR THE RECORD

FULL COMMITTEE HEARING NOTICE
COMMITTEE ON FOREIGN AFFAIRS
U.S. HOUSE OF REPRESENTATIVES
WASHINGTON, DC 20515-6128

Edward R. Royce (R-CA), Chairman

July 13, 2016

TO: MEMBERS OF THE COMMITTEE ON FOREIGN AFFAIRS

You are respectfully requested to attend an OPEN hearing of the Committee on Foreign Affairs, to be held in Room 2172 of the Rayburn House Office Building (and available live on the Committee website at http://www.ForeignAffairs.house.gov):

DATE: Wednesday, July 13, 2016

TIME: 10:00 a.m.

SUBJECT: Countering the Virtual Caliphate: The State Department's Performance

WITNESS: The Honorable Richard Stengel
Under Secretary for Public Diplomacy and Public Affairs
U.S. Department of State

By Direction of the Chairman

The Committee on Foreign Affairs seeks to make its facilities accessible to persons with disabilities. If you are in need of special accommodations, please call 202/225-5021 at least four business days in advance of the event, whenever practicable. Questions with regard to special accommodations in general (including availability of Committee materials in alternative formats and assistive listening devices) may be directed to the Committee.

COMMITTEE ON FOREIGN AFFAIRS
MINUTES OF FULL COMMITTEE HEARING

Day **Wednesday** Date **7/13/2016** Room **2172**

Starting Time **10:10** Ending Time **11:50**

Recesses **0** (___to___) (___to___) (___to___) (___to___) (___to___) (___to___)

Presiding Member(s)
Chairman Edward R. Royce, Rep. Jeff Duncan

Check all of the following that apply:

Open Session ☑   Electronically Recorded (taped) ☑
Executive (closed) Session ☐   Stenographic Record ☑
Televised ☑

TITLE OF HEARING:

Countering the Virtual Caliphate: The State Department's Performance

COMMITTEE MEMBERS PRESENT:

See attached.

NON-COMMITTEE MEMBERS PRESENT:

none

HEARING WITNESSES: Same as meeting notice attached? Yes ☑ No ☐
(If "no", please list below and include title, agency, department, or organization.)

STATEMENTS FOR THE RECORD: *(List any statements submitted for the record.)*

IFR - Rep. Lois Frankel

TIME SCHEDULED TO RECONVENE _____
or
TIME ADJOURNED **11:50**

_____
Full Committee Hearing Coordinator

HOUSE COMMITTEE ON FOREIGN AFFAIRS
FULL COMMITTEE HEARING

PRESENT	MEMBER	PRESENT	MEMBER
X	Edward R. Royce, CA	X	Eliot L. Engel, NY
	Christopher H. Smith, NJ	X	Brad Sherman, CA
X	Ileana Ros-Lehtinen, FL		Gregory W. Meeks, NY
X	Dana Rohrabacher, CA		Albio Sires, NJ
X	Steve Chabot, OH	X	Gerald E. Connolly, VA
	Joe Wilson, SC	X	Theodore E. Deutch, FL
	Michael T. McCaul, TX		Brian Higgins, NY
	Ted Poe, TX		Karen Bass, CA
X	Matt Salmon, AZ	X	William Keating, MA
	Darrell Issa, CA	X	David Cicilline, RI
	Tom Marino, PA		Alan Grayson, FL
X	Jeff Duncan, SC	X	Ami Bera, CA
X	Mo Brooks, AL		Alan S. Lowenthal, CA
	Paul Cook, CA	X	Grace Meng, NY
	Randy Weber, TX	X	Lois Frankel, FL
X	Scott Perry, PA		Tulsi Gabbard, HI
X	Ron DeSantis, FL	X	Joaquin Castro, TX
X	Mark Meadows, NC	X	Robin Kelly, IL
X	Ted Yoho, FL		Brendan Boyle, PA
	Curt Clawson, FL		
X	Scott DesJarlais, TN		
	Reid Ribble, WI		
X	Dave Trott, MI		
X	Lee Zeldin, NY		
X	Dan Donovan, NY		

43